ELLEN DYROP

HANNA KRISTINSDÓTTIR

Rediscovered
TREASURES

NEW
HOLLAND

Contents

Foreword

This book has been a glorious, fun and inspirational joint effort for us – we are both passionately interested in beautiful embroideries, old silver cutlery, nostalgic china and outworn, well-used fabrics. Where other people see old junk, we see potential treasure, and are inspired to give our rediscovered articles a new purpose and a new decorative role in our lives. We are always on the lookout for so-called junk that can be used in so many new ways to reflect our imagination, our personalities and our unusual style.

For us, re-using and revamping things has turned into a way of life, and we are captivated by the stories that these old objects have to tell. Lovely well-used artefacts with decorative details put our creative impulses into top gear.

Re-using old objects has become a popular and necessary trend in our rich part of the world – we live in an age of excess and throw away far too much. We can learn to value the objects we already possess and discover new charms within them.

We hope we can share some of the enthusiasm and pleasure in making things that we have felt while we were involved in this project. Most of all, we hope that this book will inspire you and that you, too, will find hidden treasures in search of a new life. Take a close look at what you have, begin to haunt second-hand shops, auctions or jumble sales and let yourself go.

Good luck!

Ellen and Hanna

THE KITCHEN DOOR
What better way to show where the kitchen is than hanging a large pewter spoon on the door as decoration. The decorative stencil may also be a dead giveaway! (See instructions on page 124.)

Kitchen

Dramatic door plaques

Welcome your guests in a most unusual way – unique door plaques made from old platters give your home a real personal touch.

NAMEPLATES ON A PLATTER
Old oval platters in glazed earthenware, china and silverplate are turned into decorative door plaques with the help of stencils. We have used water-based interior paint and a stencil to put the lettering on the dishes in order to create these quirky bathroom and entrance hall plaques (see instructions for stencilling on page 124).

SERVING DISH ON A DOOR
An oval serving dish is transformed into a iinique front door embellishment with the help of a plate hanger and a cut-glass prism. Glue a plate hanger to the back of the dish (available from hardware stores and china shops). The small decorative holes in the dish make it easy to add flowers and attach the prism with wire.

Kitchen creativity

The kitchen's comforting charm gives sustenance to body and soul while old kitchen utensils make a wonderful contrast to all the high-tech equipment in our modern homes.

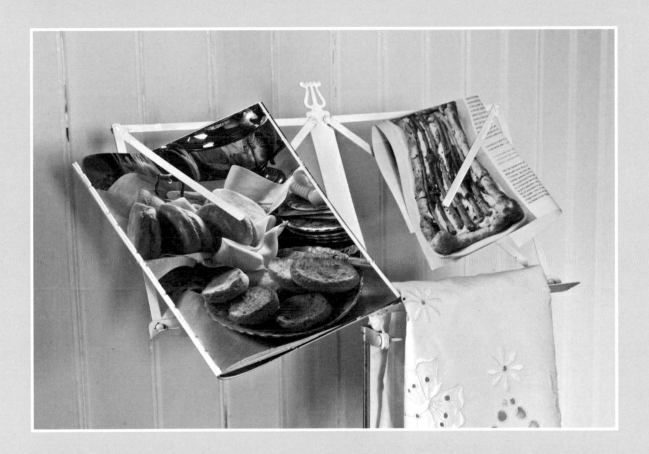

A DRAWER ON THE WORKTOP
You can easily make an extra shelf by placing an old wooden drawer on its side on your worktop. Instant storage space and instant re-use – but you could always paint it to suit your decor.

MUSICAL COOKERY BOOK STAND
Make use of an old music stand as a cookery book holder in the kitchen. We've sprayed ours with white paint and hung pretty vintage linen towels from the stand – really useful for drying your hands while you are baking.

LINEN TOWEL AS COOK'S APRON

Transform an old linen towel into a practical kitchen apron with some simple stitching. Linen towels and napkins of this type often have decorative monograms, motifs and embroidery that provides further embellishment to your project. (See page 124 for simple sewing instructions.)

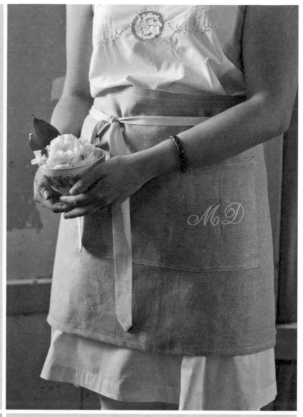

KITCHEN SUSPENSION

An old metal chandelier (right) that once held candles is suspended from the ceiling with fine chain and kitchen utensils are hung from it with S-hooks.

STILL-LIFE WITH KITCHEN UTENSILS

A beautiful salvaged gilt frame (left) with a great deal of nostalgic character has been given a new role in the kitchen. Hang S-hooks through the frame, from which you can suspend utensils, cups and even garlic. If your frame is gilt and you want to tone down the colour, paint it white with a water-based interior paint, then rub it off with a cloth before the paint is dry. Make a quick and effective pot stand by gluing champagne corks together with ceramic adhesive.

This plate rack is now used as a bookshelf
and as display for kitchen bits and pieces.

Display attractive vintage postcards and
photographs on a toast rack no longer
in use – stylish and fun.

Blackboard magic

Blackboard painting is easy! All you need is blackboard paint or black matt water-based interior paint, a brush and the articles you want to transform. Paint three coats on the item and let the paint dry before you write on it with chalk. Recipes, messages and traditional sayings look good, and can be wiped off with a damp cloth.

KITCHEN BLACKBOARD
A wall in the kitchen (left) is an ideal candidate for some blackboard paint magic – make lists, leave messages for family members and write up a recipe or two. The face of the kitchen clock is the base of a baking tin and a clockwork kit (available from craft shops). Drill a hole in the middle of the tin and mount the clockworks according to the kit instructions.

MESSAGE ON A BREADBOARD
Old, well-used wooden chopping boards past their best for culinary purposes can be turned into charming message boards. This one might make a perfect 'do not disturb' sign for your bedroom doorknob.

WORKTOP NOTICE BOARD

This attractive worktop notice board had an earlier life as a picture frame. The picture is turned into a blackboard with the help of a few coats of blackboard paint on the backing board.

COFFEE BREAK

A simple coat of blackboard paint makes it easy to write on metal containers (below). The tin can holding the yellow flowers has been given three coats of blackboard paint to transform it into a quaint and useful vase.

PAINT RIGHT ON THE TABLE

Write your recipes directly onto a tabletop painted with blackboard paint. Clever and quaint!

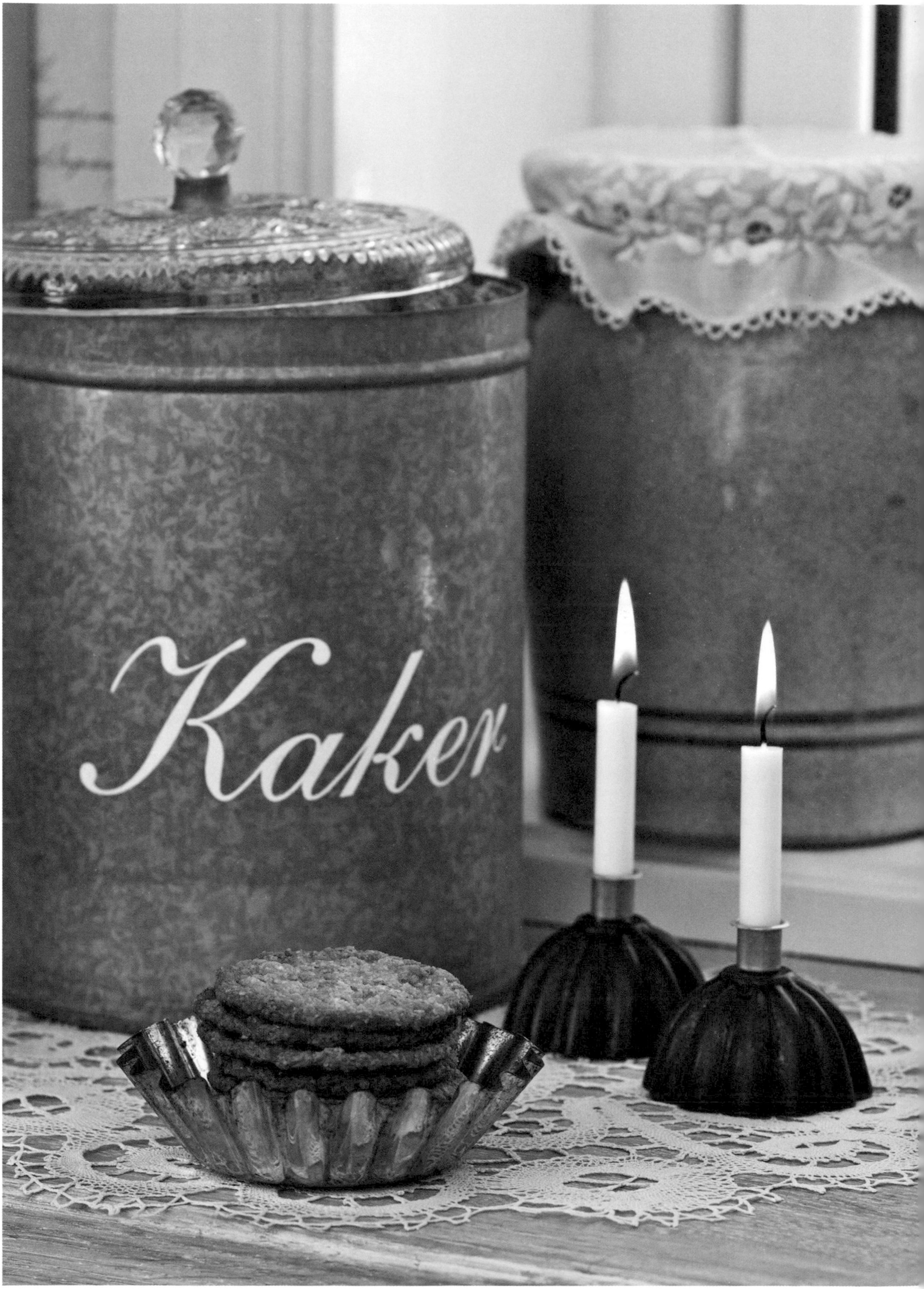
Kaker

Baking tin transformations

Baking tins and jelly moulds are often piled up in junk shops. In the past these tins were used to prepare food for special occasions but today they are more commonly used as decoration. Search out tins large and small in unusual shapes, give them a good wash, and let yourself be inspired by our ideas.

MASSES OF IDEAS

Using ceramic adhesive, fasten candle-holders on to small cake moulds that have a glorious patina of age. The large metal biscuit tin has a glass lid made from an old cut-glass serving-plate that has been given a glass knob on the top. Carefully bore a hole in the centre of the plate with a glass drill and screw a knob into place.

HAPPY BUNNY

Here we have made a pretty door-stop from plaster-of-Paris and an old metal jelly mould in the form of a very sweet rabbit. Pour the liquid plaster-of-Paris into the mould, and leave it to set. Leave the hardened plaster in the mould to weigh it down while the exterior detailing of the mould provides the metallic finish.

BAKING TIN–JELLY MOULD ROW

Baking tins and jelly moulds in various shapes look great as a decorative frieze in a kitchen or pantry (above). These have been fastened around the wall above the shelves with a glue gun.

CAKE STOP

If the doors in your house don't stay open of their own accord, then a 'plaster-cake' might be just the thing (left). Mix plaster-of-Paris powder with water following the instructions on the packet. Stir to a smooth paste, and then pour the mixture into an old decorative baking tin or jelly mould. Let the plaster set and turn out the cake to serve as your doorstop.

BAKING TINS FOR DOORKNOBS
Small, individual-sized tart and
cake tins and old silvered knobs
can be transformed into original
and unusual doorknobs for
kitchen cupboards. Drill a hole in
the tart tin to accommodate the
screw of the doorknob.

Cutlery creations

Old cutlery has beautiful decorative detail and it doesn't need to be silver to be charming. Look in second-hand shops − cutlery is often lying in heaps and sold cheaply. We have re-used cutlery in several ways: inside frames, in a wind chime and hung on a chandelier.

CUTLERY CHANDELIER
Beautiful pieces of oxidized silver cutlery are attached firmly to a metal chandelier with wire, making an unusual decorative talking-point for your dining room or kitchen.

DAMASK AND LACE CUTLERY POUCH
Should you happen to have a pretty set of silver cutlery, you might consider giving it a suitably beautiful home. A piece of lace and an old damask napkin become a lovely cutlery pouch (see page 125 for sewing instructions).

CURLY-TINED WIND CHIMES

Thread beads on a series of strings, then hang the beads on a frame (we have used part of an old candleholder, left). Bend the tines of the forks with pliers and tie them to the strings of beads, then decorate the tines with beads. Once balanced, hang the wind chimes where they will catch the eye and the breeze.

SILVER HEIRLOOMS IN A FRAME

Do you only have a few pieces of your favourite cutlery? To mount silverware in a frame (above), make sure that the backing board of the frame is of thick cardboard. Cover the cardboard with the fabric of your choice (lace and old linen here). Make fine holes through all layers and tie the cutlery with wire, fastened firmly at the back of the board.

CUTLERY ON FABRIC

Cutlery designs can be transferred (below) to tablemats, napkins or placemats with the aid of transfer paper and a printer (see page 125 for instructions on how to use transfer paper).

Cups, cookies and cupcakes

A cup usually tells a story about its owner, and in the past it was the custom to have your own cup with your name marked on it in neat lettering. In days gone by, people also distinguished between everyday cups and cups for 'best'. Fine, fragile porcelain cups were beautifully decorated, and if you are lucky, you may find some in your grandmother's cupboard or at jumble sales.

ROSECUP CHANDELIER

An informal and attractive chandelier made from old rose-patterned cups and a wrought-iron chandelier (left). The original candleholders were removed, and the chandelier was spray-painted white. Nostalgic tea cups and saucers in different rose patterns were glued firmly in place of the candleholders. Either put tea-lights into the cups, or glue metal candleholders to the base of each cup to hold taller candles.

CUP MOTIFS

Attach cup motifs from fabric remnants of contrasting colours to hand-towels using appliqué, blanket stitching around the cups (see page 126 for templates and a description of how to appliqué). The real cup, serving as a gift tag to the hand-towel, has been written on using a washable porcelain ink-marker (available in craft shops and online). The writing is fixed by baking the cup in a domestic oven at 150°C (300°F) for about 35 minutes.

CUP-SHAPED BISCUITS

An old tin lunchbox filled with homemade cup-shaped biscuits (right) make a perfect present (see page 126 for cup template). Makes 24 biscuits.

125 g (4 oz) butter
125 g (4 oz) caster sugar
1 egg
450 g (1 lb) plain flour
1 tsp baking powder
2 tbsp milk

Preheat the oven to 170°C (325°F). Cream together the butter and sugar until light. Beat in the egg, then sift the flour and baking powder together and add to the butter mixture. Add milk to make a dough, mix well, then chill for an hour. Roll out and cut cup shapes using the template. Bake at 170°C (325°F) for 15–18 minutes or until lightly golden.

SWEET ROSEBUD

Further the rose theme by decorating your cupcakes with sugar rosebuds. Whose heart wouldn't melt completely?

CUPCAKES IN A CUP

Bake in paper cases and serve in cups. Ice and decorate the cupcakes with sweets and sprinkles. This recipe makes about 12.

125 g (4 oz) butter
125 g (4 oz) caster sugar
2 eggs
125 g (4 oz) self-raising flour
1 lemon, juice and zest
Icing: 250–350 g (9–12 oz) icing sugar
2–4 tbsp water

Preheat the oven to 190°C (350°F). Cream together the butter and and sugar until light and fluffy. Beat in the eggs, one at a time. Add the lemon zest and juice and flour and beat until smooth. Pour the mixture into paper cases to three-quarters full. Bake in the centre of the oven for 12–15 minutes or until firm to the touch. Let the cakes cool. Sift the icing sugar and beat in the water, 1 tablespoon at a time, to get a smooth glossy icing. Ice and decorate as you wish and serve in charming little cups.

ROMANTIC GLASS BOWLS
We have created this elegant stemmed glass bowl by gluing a dessert bowl firmly to an old silver-plated candlestick with strong glass and china adhesive.

China and glass revamps

Jumble sales and second-hand shop expeditions may yield only one piece of each object or perhaps only a few pieces of a whole set of china or glass. Let this be an inspiration rather than a hindrance and mix together cups, candlesticks, plates and eggcups in fabulous combinations – with a bit of madness.

CELEBRATION CENTREPIECE
The cream-coloured decorated jug (above) is the perfect container for these gloriously white ranunculus. The whole ensemble – jug, silver dish and cutlery – is beautifully displayed on an old window etched with a lacy pattern. The battered frame with its worn and chipped paintwork add shabby-chic charm to an impromptu celebration setting.

CUP AND PLATE TOWER
Eggcups, plates and glass dishes are glued together to make an exuberant layered cake plate several storeys high (below and right). Note the old window frame used here as a tray.

CHEESE DOME FROM A CUT-GLASS BOWL
Drill a hole right in the middle of the base of the bowl with a glass drill. Use a light touch with the drill – don't press the drill down too hard on the glass. Screw a little knob into place, and put the dome over a plate or a small dish.

JEWELLERY ON CHINA
Cups and tea plates (right) in glorious combinations – the various parts are glued together with glass and china adhesive. This dish is suitable for holding jewellery or for serving little cakes and dainty tea-time treats.

A GREENHOUSE FROM OLD WINE GOBLETS
Large wine goblets turned upside down make excellent mini greenhouses for bulbs and cuttings. The base of each glass stem is decorated with a glass bead or little doorknob glued into place.

Glassware glamour

If you have glasses you no longer use, give them a new lease of life as mini greenhouses or candlesticks. Spring bulbs in old cut-glass vases make a beautiful and harmonious group.

SPRING BULBS IN OLD VASES AND JUGS
Narcissus and other spring bulbs displayed in a group of cut-glass and cream glass jugs create an air of springtime when arranged together on a silver tray.

CANDLESTICKS FROM OLD GLASSES
Old liqueur or small wine glasses from incomplete sets are transformed into beautiful candlesticks when glued, one on top of the other, with strong glass and china adhesive. Here the glasses are filled with dried roses and candleholders are glued on top. Use tea-lights if you don't have candleholders.

MAGIC LANTERN IN A JAR
The three screws on the
lamp-holder should be screwed
all the way in. Thread the
aluminium ring from the
preserving jar past the lamp-
holder. Slacken the screws and
let the lid rest on them. Attach
a light bulb and then screw
the preserving jar on to the
aluminium ring. Use a clear
low-wattage light bulb.

Storage jar inspirations

Storage and preserving jars come in various sizes – we love them because they are practical and can be used for almost everything. Moreover, they are beautiful on display – one jar sitting on the kitchen worktop can be decoration in itself!

'FLOATING' STORAGE JARS
Drill three holes in the aluminium ring of the jar. Attach the ring firmly with small screws to the underside of a shelf. Fill the jars with whatever you wish to store. Screw the jars into place. It's not necessary to use the glass lids that belong to the jars, since they will be airtight anyway.

NIFTY KNIFE HOLDER
Fill a preserving jar with wooden skewers to create a practical and decorative way to protect and hold kitchen knives safely.

LIGHT THROUGH LACE
These lacy candle lanterns (above) are effective when used indoors and out. Wrap some old scraps of lace tightly around a preserving jar and fasten at the back with some small stitches or adhesive.

Make the lace rosette by rolling a length of lace round, and gathering it together into shape. Use strong thread to sew the rosettes together.

Place tea-lights or candles in the jars and replace the aluminium rings before lighting the candles; don't put the glass tops back on the jars.

IMPOSING ORDER ON PAPER AND STRING
With a glass drill carefully drill a hole in the middle of the glass lid of a preserving jar (left). Don't press down hard on the drill while it's working. Put balls of string, ribbon and rick-rack in the jars and thread the ends through the holes in the lid for brilliant dispensers (right). The paperweight (right) is plaster-of-Paris cast in a baking tin, while the handle on the top of the zinc box is a glass doorknob that has been smartened up.

Set the table

Junk-shop finds such as old buckets, bottles and sheets can make a festive table setting. Invite your nearest and dearest, and set the table with cutlery and dinnerware from a scattering of services.

CELEBRATORY TABLE SETTING
Set a beautiful festive table with utilitarian objects. We've used an old monogrammed bed sheet as a tablecloth, old bottles as vases and a porcelain chamber pot as a champagne bucket (left). The chair backs are decorated with lace placemats, and the cutlery and napkins are stored in an old wire basket that had an earlier life as a milk bottle holder.

UNIQUE CHAMPAGNE BUCKET
This metal bucket (above) was well scrubbed, the interior was spray-painted white, then 'Champagne' was stencilled with white paint on the outside. Filled with ice-cubes and a few festive sprays of flowers, this charming ice bucket keeps champagne cold for ages.

DAMASK NAPKINS AS TABLE RUNNER

Join old damask napkins together with buttons
and loops of silk thread (left) to make a
splendid table runner. Join two, three or four
napkins of the same size, depending on how
long you want the table runner to be.

PILLOWCASES AS PLACE MATS

You can use old embroidered pillowcases as
placemats on the table (above). Pillowcases can
also be used as small centrepiece cloths in the
middle of the table. Note the clever use of a
clip-on candleholder on an individual plate.

Clever clockworks

Only your imagination limits what you can turn into clocks – all you need is an object, a clockwork kit and the ability to drill a hole in the object. Clockwork kits are easily fitted, and full instructions are given with the kits (available from craft and hobby shops and via the internet).

TIME FOR CAKE
Drill a hole in the lid of a decorative cake tin (left, top), then fit clockworks in place according to the kit's instructions, and display in an appropriate spot.

A lovely old rose tapestry (left, bottom) is cut into an oval shape, edged with a black silk ribbon and then glued to an oval piece of cardboard the same size as the tapestry. When the glue is dry, carefully make a hole through the tapestry and the cardboard for the clockworks kit using an awl or darning needle. Be careful when making the hole, since the the tapestry work can easily unravel.

SILVER DISH WITH HANDS
An old silver tray and a kit are all you need to create this 'sterling' revamp (above left).

A TIMELY ROSE
Using a special china and glass drill, make a hole in a rose-patterned plate to create another quaint clock (above centre).

CHINA AND LACEWORK TIMEPIECE
Drill a hole in the middle of a china plate and glue on a lace doily using wood glue, that is transparent when it dries (above right). Fit the clockworks as instructed in the kit.

Light and warmth

Candlelight creates a cosy, warm atmosphere. You can use found objects such as cake tins, cream jugs and cups as candle moulds, but watch your fingers – the liquid wax is hot!

CANDLES IN CUPS
We have made candles in a beautiful collection of old rose-patterned cups and cream jugs (left), but you can use any pretty container that takes your fancy or suits your decor. You are only limited by your imagination (see page 126 for candle-making instructions).

WARM HEART CANDLE
This larger candle with three wicks was made in an attractive heart-shaped cake tin (above). Keep your eyes peeled for pretty pieces of old china, glass, bakeware and tins when scouring junk shops. A set of tea cup or cake tin candles make a very welcome gift.

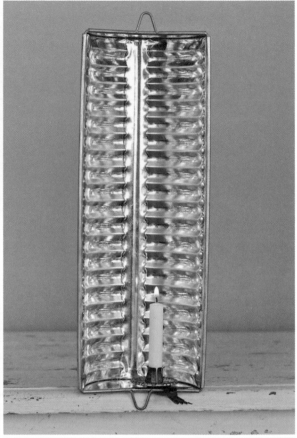

LOAF TIN CANDLESTICKS

Attach clip-on candleholders firmly to textured loaf tins. Glue a picture hook to the back of the tin in order to hang it on the wall (above left) or rest the tin on a shelf (or other flat surface). Picture hooks can be bought in framing shops, craft stores and and many DIY and hardware stores.

TEA CUP CANDLEHOLDER

A rose-shaped metal candleholder is glued firmly inside the rose-patterned cup (left) with glass and china glue to make a completely rosy creation.

LADLE IN A VASE
A lovely old silver
soup ladle rests
on a bed of coarse
sea salt in the base
of a glass vase to
create this unusual
candleholder. The
candlelight reflects
on the surrounding
cut-glass decanters,
helping to create
an atmosphere
of romance. Lift
the ladle to light
or extinguish the
candle flame.

Baskets and lampshades

Old lampshades can be revamped, re-covered and reinvented as entirely new objects to give them a whole new lease of life.

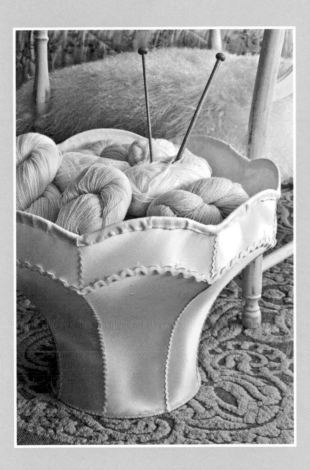

LAMPSHADE ON ITS HEAD

A very unassuming lampshade (above) is turned into a charming and useful knitting basket. We've lined the lampshade with white linen material, which covers the base of the frame so that the yarn doesn't fall through.

PRETTY BASKET TRANSFORMATION

Old lace and crochet work are threaded through a wicker basket (left) before placing it on a lamp base with an existing wire frame. Care must be taken to ensure that the light bulb doesn't come into contact with the basket.

ATMOSPHERIC CANDLESTICKS

Small decorative lampshades can be transformed in several ways. Here metal candleholders (available from craft and hobby shops) are attached to the bulb-holders on small upturned lampshades (above). Note in the background the clever use of a shade as a vase for roses (a small tin or plastic container within the shade holds the flowers and their water. Shades of all sizes can be used as decorative plant-pot holders or vases – you will need to remove the bulb-holders with pliers or wire cutters.

LAMPSHADE TO BASKET
Make a handle with steel wire or even an old
hanger and fasten it to the lampshade. Wrap
lace trimming or rickrack around the handle.
Remove the bulb-holder with pliers or wire
cutters and then create a base for the basket
with cardboard.

THERMOS FLASK LAMP BASES

Remove the glass lining from the flasks, and drill holes in the side near the base for the electric cord. A lightbulb-holder can be fixed to the neck of the thermos flask (you can buy lamp fitting in many DIY and hardware shops). For the lamp on the left, we have stripped an old lampshade and wrapped ribbon round the frame, then threaded beads on to wire and twined it round. The lampshade on the right is an old silk shade further embellished with pretty buttons, rick-rack and lace trim.

No-so-straight lace

For many years, lace and lace doilies have been considered rather old-fashioned and not worth collecting. These pretty, romantic textiles have been given some smart new twists that suit today's interiors while still exuding their own sweet charm.

CONCRETE COUNTERPLAY
A concrete candlestick is used as the stem for a lace doily basket (see page 127 for instructions on how to stiffen lace with sugar). The contrast of materials is both surprising and fun.

LACY MUFFIN BASKET
A stiffened lace doily make a sweet basket for a muffin (again, see page 127 for instructions). This clever technique can be used with other textiles as well.

PRETTY COVERS

Small crocheted doilies can be used as decorative covers for small glass containers and jars (left). Cover homemade pots of jam or jars of your own fudge or sweets with doilies and scraps of ribbon to embellish homemade presents.

BOOK COVERS

Cut out a cup motif (below) from a scrap of lacy hand-towel and appliqué to a lace tablemat with small firm stitches (see page 126 for instructions on how to appliqué). Embroider the title of the book on to the mat using simple embroidery stitches. Fix the mat to the book in the same way you would a paper cover using textile adhesive.

LACE UNDER GLASS

This serving tray (left) has been given a new lease of life with the help of some wallpaper, a lace doily and a sheet of glass. Line the tray with attractive wallpaper, place a doily in the centre and cover both with a sheet of glass to fit the tray. Serving trays can also be made from old picture-frames with drawer handles mounted on the ends. The vase was created from an empty tin covered with the same wallpaper and then decorated with lace. Cheap, cheerful and chic!

GRANNY'S OLD LACE CURTAINS
Embellish a bedcover with an edging of lace (above left). We found this lace border on the bottom section of a large curtain – the kind of sheer curtains that covered the whole window and were popular in the 1970s. Sew the lace firmly to the bedcover by hand.

LACY CLOTHES HANGER
A lace tablecloth sewn to fit a clothes hanger (above right) not only protects clothes from the metal hanger but can also be decorative in its own right. This looks pretty hung up in a bedroom or hallway.

OLD CUSHION MEETS OLD DOILY
It's so simple to revamp an old cushion (right). Sew the doily firmly to the cushion cover with small hand stitches.

'It's not how much we have, but how much we enjoy it that makes us happy.'

ELEGANT CLOTHES HANGER
We've made a beautiful bespoke clothes hanger from a pretty old blouse that has lace and buttons of mother-of-pearl. The fabric-covered hanger is particularly useful for protecting delicate dresses (see page 127 for sewing instructions).

FROM POTHOLDER TO TABLECLOTH
A collection of crocheted lace doilies and decorative potholders are transformed into a fine tablecloth. The potholders and doilies are pieced together by hand using small stitches – simple but very effective.

From functional to fabulous

Most of us have some old potholders lying around, and if not, they are easy to find in second-hand shops. Often crocheted or knitted from scraps of yarn in highly original colour combinations, they lend themselves to all sorts of treatments – we've created a colourful tea cosy, a garland, a cushion and a tablecloth.

GLORIOUS POTHOLDER CUSHION
Old potholders in a variety of styles and stitches are used to embellish a plain white linen cushion cover. Sew the potholders firmly to the cushion cover using a sewing machine, then hand-tie silk ribbon bows to the loops of the potholders. (Sewing instructions for a plain cushion cover on page 132.)

POTHOLDER GARLAND
A straw garland is covered with colourful potholders
for a quick and quaint decoration. Fasten the
potholders to the garland with pins or small stitches,
then tie ribbon bows to the loops of the potholders.

ROSY TEA COSY
For the sides, sew two potholders together over and under the spout; then tie it round the teapot with ribbon at the top and bottom of the handle. The lid is covered by a circular potholder then threaded with a ribbon round the edge. Tie the ribbon in a bow to secure it in place.

Take notice

Magnets can be made out of almost anything, as long as the object is not too heavy – we've used everything from kitchen utensils to chess pieces. Noticeboards can be magnetic, but you can also make them out of cork or strong cardboard covered in fabric or embroidery, using drawing pins or tacks to attach mementos and messages.

KITCHEN MAGNETS
Baking tins, teaspoons (left) and champagne corks (above) are all light objects to which you can glue small magnets. An old distressed frame and a piece of magnetic metal make a perfect noticeboard (left) and an old tray serves the same purpose (above and right).

CHECKMATE
Here magnets are glued firmly to black and white chess pieces, providing an imaginative way to display old postcards and memorabilia on a decorative metal tray.

FADED CHARM
This beautiful screen from a bygone era becomes an unusual repository of memories. The button badges are covered in lace to create magnets. Remove the fastening pins with pliers, glue small circles of lace onto the badges with adhesive, then glue a small magnet to the back of each button.

AUNT ANNE'S SERVING TRAY

This charming serving tray with its patina of age is reinvented as a noticeboard for nostalgic postcards. The tray is hung on a plate hook and pretty silk rosebuds have been glued to small magnets with china and glass adhesive.

TABLECLOTH NOTICEBOARD

An embroidered tablecloth is folded and pinned to an artist's canvas stretcher to create a decorative noticeboard. Drawing pins or dressmaking pins can be used to attach favourite photographs and postcards.

BRASS WALL LAMP HOOK
This brass wall lamp has been stripped of its shade and electric fittings, then sprayed with primer and matt white paint in order to give it a new life as a decorative wall hook.

Hooks for everything

Make decorative and practical hooks out of anything – we've used everything from cutlery and glass knobs to wall lamps.

DOOR FRAME WITH HOOKS

We fell in love with the finish on this battered old door frame and transformed it into a useful place to hang coats and bags. We made a row of hooks by attached glass knobs at regular intervals along the frame.

SILVER HANG-UPS

Bend old pieces of cutlery then drill holes using a drill specially suited to metal, and attach the pieces to a suitable spot with screws. Items of cutlery with beautiful monograms and patterns make especially decorative hooks.

BRODERIE ANGLAISE BAG
This charming bag, from a broderie anglaise table runner, would make a pretty pyjama case or storage for delicate lingerie (see page 128 for sewing instructions). The flap of the bag threads through the back of a chair to make it a hanging case.

Bags for bits and pieces

We all have the clutter of newspapers and magazines lying around our homes. With attractive baskets and stylish embroidered fabric bags, you can find a place for all those odds and ends.

BASKET FOR PAPERS AND POST
An old cycling basket is hung from the back of a kitchen chair to provide a useful place for the daily paper and the post.

MAGAZINE HOLDER
Corners from an embroidered tablecloth are sewn to make a decorative bag for magazines. The bag hangs on the back of a chair, but mustn't be so overloaded that the chair topples over. (See page 128 for sewing instructions.)

ODD CHINA AND CRYSTAL LIDS

Don't worry if the bottom part of a covered dish or bowl gets broken and you are left with a spare lid. Give these often beautiful lids a new role as a top to a wicker basket (far left and left), covering a plant pot or embellishing a wallpapered tin.

AN ORIGINAL COFFEE TABLE

A wicker trunk (right), to which we have added metal legs, becomes an attractive coffee table with the added bonus of storage for magazines and all the paraphernalia of busy family life. You can also use wooden legs from old tables and chests of drawers.

TAPESTRY TROLLEY
Here we have revamped a
worn-out shopping trolley
and given it a new bag
made from old tapestry
and linen fabrics. We took
apart the old bag and and
used the pieces to make
a pattern for a new bag.
Using a patchwork of
tapestry, unbleached linen
and gingham cotton, we
constructed the new bag
with the help of the pattern
(sewing instructions on
page 130).

Basket and bag embellishments

Decorate handbags and baskets with small tapestry embroideries, lace and buttons. Embellish your basket to give it your personal stamp or sew a new handbag or shopping trolley out of scraps of old fabric.

TAPESTRY ON A BASKET
A little tapestry cushion cover is unstitched and fastened to a handled basket with rustic pewter buttons on the corners (above left).

HANDBAG FROM BLANKET AND LACE
An attractive handbag with wooden handles is sewn from an old woollen blanket and lace (above centre). Wooden handles can be salvaged from junk shop finds or bought in craft shops (see page 129 for instructions).

LACY BASKET
A well-used basket with handles (top right) is customized by lining it with white linen and decorating the outside with lace and crocheted doilies. The inside pocket was made from an old embroidery picture and can be opened and closed with two buttons.

CHARMING EARTHENWARE BOWL AND JUG
Decoupage can dramatically transform
the appearance of everyday objects. The
brilliant blue flower motifs were taken from
a patterned paper napkin and transferred
to a plain white bowl and jug (see page 130
for instructions).

Decorative decoupage

A very old decorative technique using paper, glue and varnish, decoupage provides endless creative possibilities. Here, patterned paper napkins are used to give old objects a completely new look.

LONG STEM ROSES
The base of the stem on these old glasses is decorated with rose motifs from a paper napkin (see page 130 for decoupage instructions). Finish by painting the inside base of the glass stem with white water-resistant paint over the decoupage, which then allows the motif to be seen more clearly.

GLASS PRISM WITH MOTIF
Using the same decoupage technique, decorate a glass prism and hang up to display (see page 130 for decoupage instructions).

PATCHWORK WITH WALLPAPER

A slightly shabby kitchen stool (right) is given a facelift with scraps of different wallpaper patterns arranged in a patchwork design on the seat, transforming it into a charming bedside table. A small baking tin was made into a candlestick by gluing a candleholder on to it with glass and china adhesive, while the beautiful rose-patterned china cup is perfect for holding small bits of jewellery overnight.

DOMED DECOUPAGE TRAY

This glass bowl (above) has been transformed into a cut-glass dome with a glass doorknob as a handle. Carefully drill a hole in the bowl with a glass drill and screw on the knob. The metal tray beneath has been decoupaged using rose-patterned paper napkins. (See page 130 for decoupage instructions.)

OLD SHADE GETS NEW LIFE

The inside of the glass shade from this old hanging lamp has been decoupaged with large floral motifs for a delicate and pretty revamp. (See page 130 for decoupage instructions.)

ROSY CHEST OF DRAWERS

We rubbed white furniture wax on to the chest of drawers (left) and then polished it with a soft cloth before finally decorating each drawer with pages from a book about roses. The pages are stuck on with decoupage adhesive and painted over with varnish. The walls have also been covered with pages from the same book. (See page 130 for decoupage instructions.)

ROSE CONTAINERS

Conjure up the finest jars for the table by saving tin cans in different sizes. These have many practical uses, and because tins are completely watertight, they also make super flower vases. And it couldn't be simpler − cut rose-patterned wallpaper (or pages from a book) to the appropriate width and fasten to the tin with tape or glue for instant chic.

Family pictures

Who doesn't have treasured family pictures lying in albums and drawers? Bring them out and show them in a new and original way.

HAPPY MEMORIES
A great way to show off family pictures is to print them on photo paper and stick them on to beautiful china or pewter plates or old tins (left). We have used adhesive pads on the backs of the photos so they can be removed if the plates are needed for another purpose later.

FAMILY PICTURES ON A CUSHION
We have transferred a cherished family photo on to a white linen cushion (above) with the help of transfer sheets and a printer. White and cream buttons in different sizes and styles are used to create a frame. (See page 125 for instructions on using transfer sheets and printer.)

Old hang-ups

Coat hangers are simple domestic objects with many possibilities – transform into a row of rosy pegs, a kitchen roll or string holder and any number of other useful articles.

DECORATIVE COAT HANGER
Strips of fabric or silk ribbon are twined round the hanger and the hook, then embellished with a bow (left), making it a perfect hanger for delicate dresses and nightgowns.

COAT HANGER MEMORIES
Attach eyelet screws at regular intervals across a wooden coat hanger (above). Thread a cord through each alternate eyelet screw and clothes peg. These paper roses from a string of broken electric lights were calling out for re-use; the flowers are attached with a glue gun, and the mementos hung from the clothes pegs.

STRING AND KITCHEN ROLL HOLDERS
We have snipped a wire coat hanger with a pair of pliers and bent two hook shapes that clip together so the kitchen roll and ball of string can be replaced easily (above left and right).

COAT HANGER IN THE KITCHEN
Using a pair of pliers, several hooks are bent into a wire coat hanger, providing excellent hooks from which to hang useful kitchen utensils (left). Embellish the hanger with colourful ribbons or string.

CHILD'S SKIRT AS PEG BAG
Sew the skirt together along the bottom hem, fill it with clothes pegs and hang the bag on a hanger in the laundry room, ready for use (right). Some of the clothes pegs are embellished with rose motif decoupage (see page 130 for decoupage instructions).

The sewing room

The sewing room is always a source of inspiration – we've made sewing boxes and pincushions from unexpected objects as well as pocket hangers for storing sewing equipment.

TIDY SEWING BOX

We have used a cardboard egg carton as a small sewing box (left). A swatch of fabric is glued to the inside line to serve as a needle and pin holder, while the egg cups provide a place thread, ribbon and tape measure. Small holes serve as slots for scissors and other tools.

WALLPAPERED SHOEBOXES

Shoeboxes are useful for storing bits and pieces and can be very pretty when covered with spare wallpaper. A well-covered shoebox also makes a beautiful gift container – the wallpaper is glued to the boxes, the edges folded inside and the outside edge is decorated with buttons.

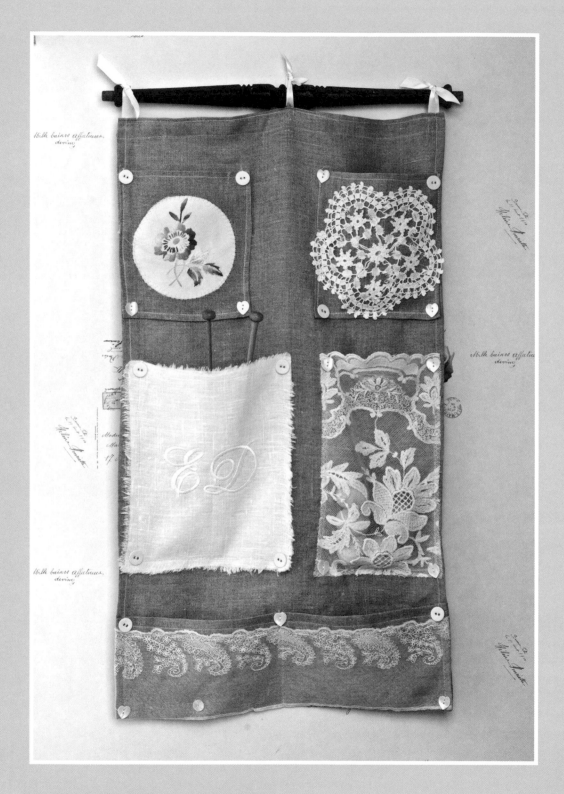

POCKET HANGER FOR THE SEWING ROOM

The pockets are made from beautiful pieces of linen, lace and doilies sewn firmly on to a linen backing. Sew mother-of-pearl buttons to the corners for decoration and make ties or hanging loops from silk ribbon. Attach the pockets to a chair leg or an old banister spindle, then hang on the wall.

PINCUPS

Small cushions made of lace fabric and filled with wadding
become practical and pretty pincushions when placed inside
rose-patterned tea cups and sugar bowls.

Mirror, mirror

Mirrors create life in a room; sometimes the surface of an old mirror is worn, giving it a beautiful antique look. Small mirrors have many decorative uses – make several wall mirrors from pretty plates and hang them together in a collage of light and pattern.

MIRROR, MIRROR ON THE WALL...
Have the cups been broken and you have only the saucers left? Glue a series of small round mirrors to pretty saucers and plates using glass and china adhesive (left). Small mirrors can be purchased in craft and hobby shops.

ROSES THROUGH THE LOOKING GLASS
Rub the back of the mirror with fine sandpaper where you would like a motif or picture to show through (above). It is easiest to achieve this worn effect on older mirrors where the silvering isn't adhering well. Stick the motif on with tape.

Gifts for friends

Good friends like to spoil each other and homemade gifts are always fun to give and receive. Delight a friend with a beautiful cup of delicious coffee beans, a key ring of buttons or a homemade loaf of bread wrapped in a lovely antique tablecloth.

FRESH BREAD
Use a small tablecloth or large placemat to wrap a home-baked loaf, and give it to someone who appreciates both. A decorative old butter knife makes a great companion piece.

LITTLE BOXES, TINY BOXES...
Print out nostalgic black-and-white pictures and glue them to the lids of little cardboard boxes. These make great gift boxes and are pretty presents in their own right.

A WARM CUDDLY COVER
Pastel fabric from an old woollen blanket is used to make a warm cuddly cover for a hot-water bottle (above left). Cut out the pieces, and machine- or hand-embroider a monogram to the front piece. (See page 131 for sewing instructions.)

GIFT FOR A COFFEE LOVER
Fill an good old china cup and saucer with coffee beans (above right) and wrap it up with cellophane and a scrap of lace for a coffee-loving friend. A beautiful silver spoon (a junk-shop find) makes a great addition to this thoughtful gift.

BUTTONS IN ABUNDANCE
So simple! Stick an attractive assortment of light-coloured buttons on to a matchbox with a glue gun for a quick little present.

DON'T COUNT THE BUTTONS
Thread buttons on to three strands of
fine wire to make a decorative key ring.
Thread the three wires through two
larger buttons and twist to create the
top of the key ring. Leave enough wire
behind the large buttons so that you can
attach a key to the key ring.

TAPESTRY ON A TIN

Make a box for small treasures by gluing a little tapestry embroidery to the lid of a tin box (left). We have first sewn the corners of the tapestry and then stuck it firmly to the lid with a fabric adhesive.

FLOWERY CHANGE PURSE

The motif from an embroidered tablecloth is used to make this small bag, which is attached to a purse clasp with small hand stitches (above). Purse clasps can be bought at craft and hobby shops (see page 131 for instructions).

'Great thoughts come from the heart.'

– MICHEL DE MONTAIGNE –

ROSE HEART
Bend a wire coathanger into a heart shape, then attach green moss and dried roses to it with twine or wire. The finishing touch is the zinc heart suspended in the middle.

Hearts and flowers

The heart is a universally meaningful symbol, but above all is symbolic of love. Our hearts are made from metal coathangers and steel wire, dried roses and old damask tablecloths.

STEEL WIRE HEARTS

Prisms from an old lamp and beads from a string of pearls are put to good use on our homemade hearts (above). Shape the steel wire (or even coathangers) into three uneven hearts with loops and squiggles. Attach the prisms to the hearts at irregular intervals, then thread the beads on to finer wire and fasten to the hearts in a random fashion.

FRAGRANT PILLOW HEART

Using the template on page 132, make a pattern the size you want then cut out a double piece of fabric. Embroider the monogram, sew on buttons and decorate with lace before you sew the heart pieces together. Fill with wadding and rose-petal pot pourri, then sew the opening by hand. Make a hanger with buttons on a strong thread (see page 132 for instructions).

Cosy cushions and throws

You can make cushion covers out of almost anything! We've used old sugar bags, tapestries and woollen blankets.

WARMTH FOR FROZEN GIRLS
Give an old softly coloured woollen blanket a new lease of life by edging it with remnants of linen and silk fabric (left). We used material from a sample book that we got from a furniture upholsterer's – shops often replace their sample books after each season. Perhaps you will be lucky if you ask nicely.

EMBROIDERED BELL PULLS
Curtain remnants in old-fashioned patterns and embroidered bell pulls are joined together to make these splendidly patterned oblong cushion covers (above).

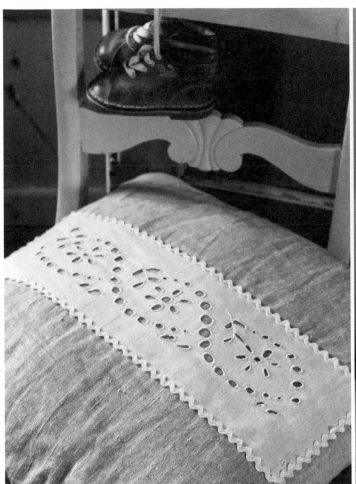

LINEN CUSHION WITH BRODERIE ANGLAISE

The broderie anglaise strip is sewn firmly on to the cushion cover using a sewing machine (above left), then the raw cut edges of the strip are covered with white rickrack braid. (See page 132 for sewing instructions for plain cushion covers.)

A SOFT SUGAR SACK

Old flour and sugar sacks have a special charm and lend themselves to all sorts of uses. This sugar sack from Cuba (above right) was machine-washed before it was transformed into a large cushion cover.

SOFT HEART CUSHION

We made a sweet heart-shaped cushion (left) from odd scraps of lace, fabric and embroidery sewn together in a patchwork pattern (see instructions on page 132).

MONOGRAMMED CUSHION

Sew an embroidered monogram from an old linen tablecloth or napkin to a cushion along with spare white buttons for further embellishment (right). You can create your own personal monogram by machine or by hand and attach it in the same way.

Floor show

The floor is an important feature of any room. Decorated tiles and wallpapered floors offer new possibilities and old wooden floors are cosy to walk on when covered with a patchwork tapestry rug.

TAPESTRIES ON THE FLOOR
The tapestries were removed from their glass frames and joined together to make a patchwork floor rug (left). The rug is lined and edged with hard-wearing linen material. It's a good idea to put a non-slip mat underneath a rug, especially on slippery wooden floors.

CROCHETED BEDCOVER TO WOVEN RUG
A light and delicate woven rug has had crocheted motifs from an unused bedcover superimposed on it, creating a pretty piece of floor covering. The motifs can be sewn in place by hand or by sewing machine.

WALLPAPER AS FLOOR COVERING
Wallpaper the floor as you would a wall. Let the
wallpaper dry before applying several coats of protective
matt floor varnish. Test a piece of the wallpaper first to
see if the pattern will withstand the varnish.

LACY TILES

Place a lace doily on the floor tile, and spray with white spray paint. Take care not to spray too much over the edges. Remove the lace doily carefully and leave behind a beautiful lacy print on the floor.

Time for tea

Afternoon tea or a cup of coffee in the morning is a must for many people. Delicate rose-patterned cups and snug tea and cup cosies keep in the warmth and create a lovely, homely atmosphere.

FROM PLACE MAT TO TEA COSY

The starting point for this tea cosy (left) is an oval embroidered placemat in white work with a narrow lace edging. The placemat is folded and cut across the middle, then sewn together with a cotton wadding lining. You could make a cosy for a cafétiere in much the same way (see page 134 for cutting and sewing instructions).

COFFEE CUP COVER

Sew a cover for your coffee cup from a old damask tablecloth. The cover is ideal for cafétieres too, if you scale it up. Play around with the remnants of ribbon, rickrack and buttons you have to hand in order to make the pretty decorative border (see page 133 for cutting and sewing instructions).

STOOL AS TEA TABLE
We've used a battered old
stool as an extra tea table,
and a beautiful silver tray
with handles is turned into
a useful shelf suspended
between the lower braces.
A lacy placemat, some
pretty rose-patterned cups
and a silver tea service
complete the picture.

HAT TEA COSY

A knitted hat is transformed into a snug tea cosy by making openings for the handle and spout. Before cutting the handle and spout openings, machine-stitch two seams side-by-side where each opening will be. Then cut a slit between the seams, and sew the edges using a zigzag stitch. Fold the cut edges over and secure with tiny hand stitches.

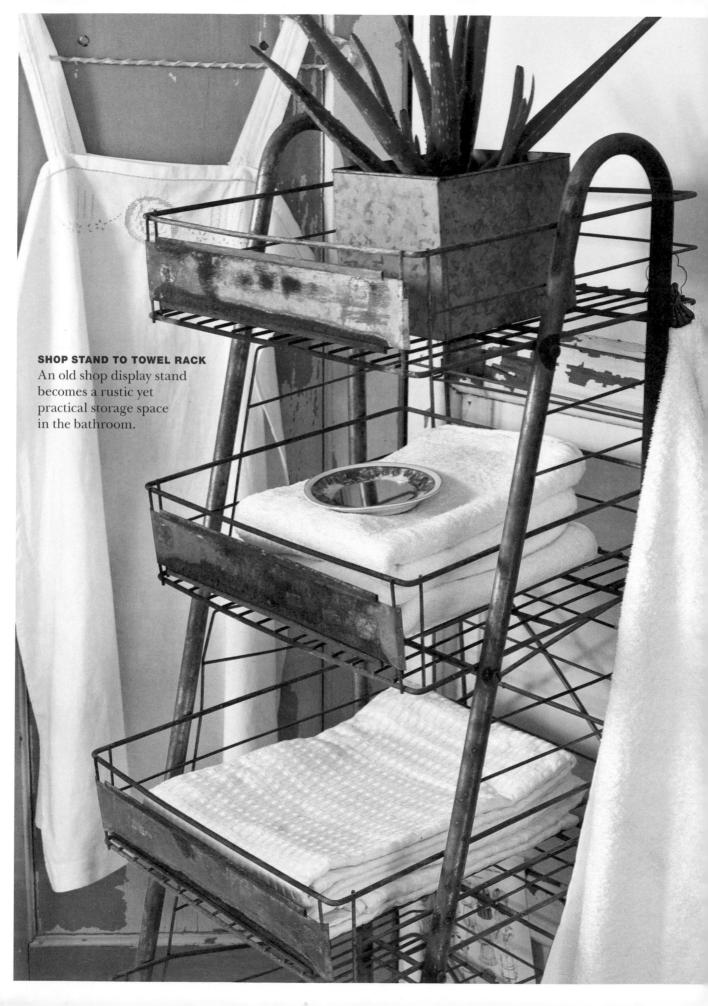

SHOP STAND TO TOWEL RACK
An old shop display stand
becomes a rustic yet
practical storage space
in the bathroom.

Bathtime pleasures

We need a lot of storage space to keep the bathroom tidy. Toiletries can be stored in old pans and baskets, while imaginative hangers and delicious scents play a part in creating the right atmosphere.

GORGEOUS SCENTS

Scented salts in a sugar bowl: mix coarse sea salt with rose-perfumed oil and red soap colouring. For perfumed oil, mix almond oil or a neutral oil, rose-perfumed oil and red soap colouring. Stand a bunch of wooden skewers in an old vinegar bottle containing the perfumed oil and they will soak up the scent. Turn the sticks and a new burst of fragrance will fill the room.

SOAP DISH TRICKS

Put a pretty old earthenware colander inside an enamelled pan to hold your soaps and nail brushes. Result: dry soaps and brushes.

FISH KETTLE AS BATH TIDY
An old fish kettle makes a great catch-all for bathroom essentials. Pour perfumed liquid soap into old milk and drinks bottles ready for bathtime; roll up small hand towels and washcloths and store in a cup.

ORIGINAL HANG-UPS
A brass handle from a chest of drawers, a small lace doily or a simple ribbon with a button all do the trick as hanging loops for hand towels and washclothes.

INSTRUCTIONS

'Have nothing in your house that you do not know to be useful, or believe to be beautiful.'

– WILLIAM MORRIS –

STENCIL PAINTING
(pages 8, 9, 45, 119, 120)

You will need: Stencil; ice-scraper; hobby paint, interior paint, fabric paint or undercoat paint; paintbrush with stiff short bristles or a small sponge

Method
1. Remove the thick paper from the back of the stencil.
2. Draw or mark guidelines with a pencil where the stencil is to be placed on the wall, floor, door or container etc.
3. Smooth the stencil on to the surface using an ice-scraper and the palm of your hand.
4. Remove the white, thin foil that covers the surface of the stencil.
5. Paint over the stencil. For small areas inside the letters, use a brush or a small sponge. Don't use too much paint at a time, and make sure that it is not too runny either. The paint can easily creep under the stencil and form uneven edges.
6. Peel the stencil off carefully.
7. Remove the remnants of foil from inside the letters with a hobby-knife or a scalpel.

COOK'S APRON FROM LINEN TOWEL
(page 12)

You will need: Linen towel; 3 metres (10 ft) ribbon; placemat or linen napkin with a monogram for a pocket

Method
1. Cut the placemat to the size required for the pocket, and if possible, let the top edge follow one of the seams on the mat.
2. Fold in the cut edge round the rest of the pocket, place the pocket on the linen towel where you want it, then sew the pocket firmly on to the linen towel.
3. Cut the ribbon into two pieces and sew a piece to either end of the top edge of the apron using firm hand stitches to make the tie strings.

Patterns: The pattern pieces are drawn without any measurements unless otherwise indicated. Use a photocopier to enlarge the patterns to the required size.

CUTLERY POUCH
(page 25)

You will need: Damask napkin; lace oddments or remnants; silk ribbon

Method
1. Cut a piece of lace the same size as the top edge of the napkin. Fold over the cut edges of the lace and sew it firmly to the napkin.
2. Fold the napkin in two so that you make a deep pouch to hold the cutlery (see the larger photograph on page 25 for a more detailed view). Sew the sides of the napkin together.
3. Sew three or four seams across the length of the napkin to form individual pockets (see illustration below).
4. Attach the silk ribbon to the napkin. Now you can roll the napkin up with the cutlery inside, and use the ribbon to tie a bow.

USING TRANSFER PAPER AND A PRINTER
(page 27, 87)

You will need: Transfer paper for light material (can be bought in hobby and craft shops)

Method
1. Place the transfer paper in the printer's paper tray, taking care that the print will appear on the white side of the sheet. Set the printer to transfer print, i.e. mirror image, and print the image.
2. Cut out the picture from the transfer paper with a margin around the image.
3. Pre-heat an iron for 5 minutes at full heat setting. **NB** Do not use steam setting!
4. Iron the fabric to which you plan to apply the transfer so that any creases are removed.
5. Place the transfer paper with the print side facing the fabric.
6. Place the fabric on a hard surface and iron with even movements.
7. Keep ironing for 3 minutes if you are transferring a whole page and 1 minutes for a half-page. When you have finished, wait for about a minute before peeling the backing paper off carefully.

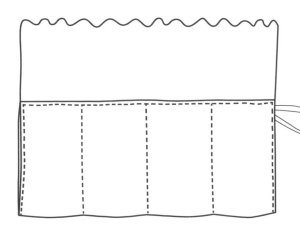

APPLIQUÉ
(page 29, 61)

You will need: Motif or drawing; fabric remnants; bonding web; fine yarn; embroidery needle; scissors; iron

Method
1. Draw the motif on the backing paper of the bonding web.
2. Place the bonding web on the wrong side of the fabric remnant and iron in place.
3. Cut out the motif, then remove the backing paper. Iron again to fix.
4. Fix the motif to the towel using blanket stitch or other simple embroidery stitch.

MAKING CANDLES
(page 50)

You will need: Containers to serve as candle holders such as old tea cups; candle wax; paraffin; wicks; two saucepans or double saucepan for *bain marie*

Method
1. Make a mixture of 30% wax and 70% paraffin. Put the mixture into a pan, and melt it over another pan of hot water on the stove. The pot containing the wax mixture must not be placed directly on the cooking ring or gas flame, since the mixture is highly flammable.
2. Place the wicks inside the cups or containers, taking care that the wick is in the centre of the container. Suspend the wick from a small stick or skewer across the top of the cup to ensure that its top stays above the level of the wax.
3. When the wax is melted, carefully pour the warm mixture into the cups.
4. When the wax has set, the candle is ready to be used.

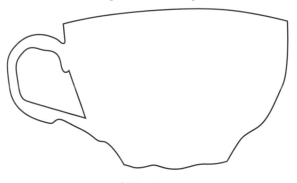

CUP MOTIFS

STIFFENING LACE WITH SUGAR SYRUP
(pages 58–59)

You will need: Saucepan; sugar; water; lace doily or whatever you chose to stiffen

Method
1. Make a sugar syrup in the saucepan by boiling together 1 part water to 2 parts sugar.
2. Allow the syrup to cool slightly before placing the lace in the syrup. Press it down well for a couple of minutes to allow the fibres to absorb the syrup.
3. Lift the lace out of the pan carefully.
4. Place the lace over an upturned saucer, cup, glass or bowl so that the lace is covering the underside of the vessel.
5. Let the lace dry before removing it from the saucer or whatever you have chosen to use as a mould.

ELEGANT CLOTHES HANGER
(page 63)

You will need: A clothes hanger, either wood or wire; an old lace blouse

Method
1. Draw a pattern in the shape of a clothes hanger. Lay the pattern over the blouse and cut a front and back piece from the lacy part of the blouse.
2. With right sides facing, stitch the pieces together, leaving a small gap at the top for the hook of the hanger. Also leave the bottom open so that you can slip the clothes hanger inside the blouse.
3. Once the hanger is in position, stitch across the bottom of the pieces to enclose the hanger.

BRODERIE ANGLAISE BAG
(page 74)

You will need: an oblong embroidered table runner or similar piece of lacy linen

Method
Fold the cloth in two (see below) with right sides together, so that you form a bag with the embroidery folded over into a flap. Sew the sides together, turn the right way out and press the seams well. You can use the flap to hang the bag over the back of a chair.

MAGAZINE HOLDER
(page 75)

You will need: an embroidered tablecloth with lace edges; checked fabric or ribbon for the ties

Method
From the tablecloth cut two corners the same size. Sew the sides of these together to form a large pouch, leaving a gap at the top. Fold the top edges over twice to form a neat hem, and sew by machine or by hand. Attach a ribbon to each side of the bag so that it can be tied to the back of a chair.

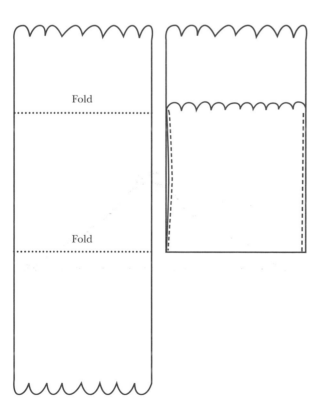

HANDBAG FROM BLANKET AND LACE
(page 79)

You will need: Woollen blanket or similar fabric remnants; lace, ribbon or rick rack; linen fabric for lining; wooden handles

Method

1. Using the templates opposite, enlarge with a photocopier to the size you want to obtain your pattern pieces. Use the pattern to cut out the required number of pieces you need in the woollen and linen fabrics.
2. Sew the lace and ribbon to the front piece of woollen fabric as indicated in the photograph, then sew zigzag stitches round the lace.
3. Sew the front and back woollen pieces to the wedge-shaped piece of woollen fabric to form the base and sides of the bag.
4. Construct and sew the lining in a similar way.
5. Attach the lining by placing the right sides of the woollen bag and the lining together and stitching around the top of the bag, leaving a small opening so that the work can be turned right side out.
6. Turn the material right side out so that the lining is on the inside of the bag. Press all of the seams well.
7. Sew up the opening by hand, and sew reinforcing stitching around the bag.
8. Sew the ribbon firmly on to the bag where the handles will go, and then tie the handles tightly to the bag with the ribbons.

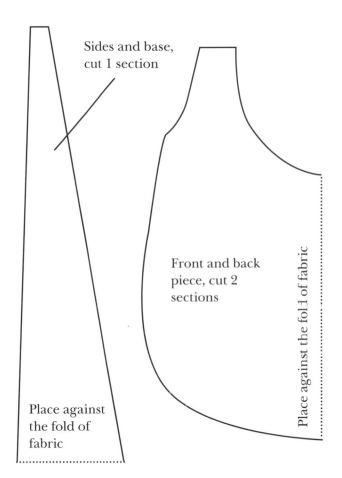

Sides and base, cut 1 section

Front and back piece, cut 2 sections

Place against the fold of fabric

Place against the fold of fabric

TAPESTRY SHOPPING TROLLEY
(page 78)

You will need: Old shopping trolley; heavy linen fabric; old tapestries; checked fabric; rope or strong cord; hooks

Method
1. Take the old trolley apart, and cut out a paper pattern for the bag and lid using the old pieces as a template. Retain the wheeled frame and base plate from the bottom of the old bag.
2. Using old tapestries and linen fabric, construct and sew a patchwork that when completed matches the paper pattern of the bag. You should have a long rectangular patchwork, allowing for a 2 cm (1 in) seam allowance. Cut out the lid from a piece of tapestry. Cut out a lining for the bag and lid from the linen using the pattern pieces as a guide, allowing for a 2 cm (1 in) seam allowance. Sew the patchwork rectangle of the bag along the short edge with right sides. Do the same with the lining. Press the seams. Place the lid and lid lining sections with right sides together, and sew along the curved section of the lid. Turn right sides out and press the seams.
3. Place the sections of the bag, one inside the other with right sides together, so that the seam is in the middle of the back when you turn the bag right side out. Then sew the lid on to the bag.
4. Fold in the bottom edge of the bag and sew it by machine. Attach the hooks along the top edge. Staple the bag firmly to the base plate.
5. Tie the bag to the frame using the rope, and thread the rope or cord through the hooks.

DECOUPAGE
(pages 80–85, 91)

Decoupage is an old decorative technique using motifs cut from magazines, wrapping paper, wallpaper or the like. These are glued firmly to an object, and then covered with varnish to create a decorative finish. You can obtain decoupage glues and varnish to use on different surfaces – wood, terracotta, glass, china, fabric and also for outdoor use. In this instance we have used motifs taken from paper napkins.

You will need: Napkins or other source of motif; water-soluable glue (PVA glue) and varnish (available from craft stores); paintbrush, scissors and a hobby knife; objects you want to decorate

Method
1. Some napkins are made of several layers of paper. In that case remove all of the lower layers so that you are left with only the top layer of paper on which the motif is printed.
2. Spread the decoupage adhesive directly on to the object to be decorated with a paintbrush and place the motif or the napkin on top.
3. Smooth carefully over the motif, and press out any air bubbles.
4. Let the motif dry.
5. With a craft knife cut or carve away any paper sticking up at the edges.
6. Paint over the motif with several layers of decoupage varnish.

WARM CUDDLY COVER
(page 100)

You will need: Woollen blanket; hot water bottle

Method
Draw round a hot water bottle to create your pattern, leaving a seam allowance. Cut a front section taking into consideration an overlap at the bottom section. Make sure that the overlap coincides with a blanket-stitched outside edge of the blanket. The back section should be cut about 5 cm (2 in) shorter than the front section. Place the pieces with right sides together, with the overlap section placed between the layers. Sew around the edges and turn right side out.

SWEET LITTLE PURSE
(page 103)

You will need: A small doily or tray cloth with an embroidered motif; fabric for lining; a purse clasp (available from craft stores)

Method
Mark the pattern to the size you want on the wrong side of the doily or tray cloth and the lining. Cut out a double layer. Sew together the outer layer and lining separately, with right sides together in each case. Turn out the outer fabric and put the lining inside. Sew the purse to the clasp with small hand stitches.

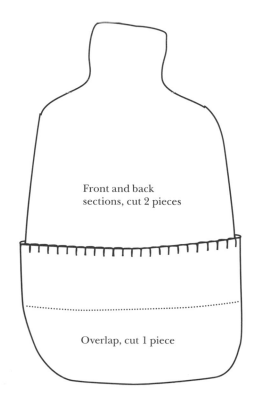

Front and back
sections, cut 2 pieces

Overlap, cut 1 piece

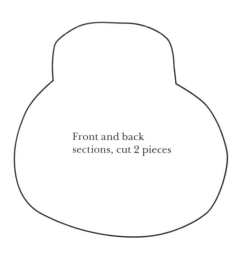

Front and back
sections, cut 2 pieces

HEART CUSHIONS
(pages 105, 108)

You will need: Buttons; old tablecloth or scraps of fabrics; pieces of lace or embroidery; polyester stuffing or wadding

Method
Draw out the heart pattern to the size you want and cut out from fabric folded in two. Embroider monograms or sew on buttons and decorate with lace or patchwork before you sew the two pieces together, with right sides facing. Leave a small opening for the filling. Turn right side out and fill with wadding. Stitch the opening by hand, and make a ribbon or button loop to attach to the cushion.

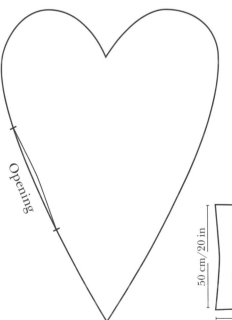

CUSHION COVERS
(pages 65, 107–109)

You will need: Fabric (about 50 x 115 cm/ 20 x 45 in); 2 buttons. We've used an old sugar sack in the above picture, but any remnants of fabric will work just as well

Method
1. Cut out a piece of fabric to the required size (see the illustration below as a guide only).
2. Fold a narrow flap under and a 5 cm (2 in) broad flap over along the short edge on the wrong side of the fabric for the buttonholes, and a 2 cm (1 in) overlap where the buttons will go. Sew the flaps by machine.
3. Sew the buttonholes by hand or machine. Decorate the fabric with monograms, embroidery, print transfer motifs or whatever you like.
4. Fold the material in two with right sides out so that it measures 50 x 50 cm (20 x 20 in). Sew on the buttons and fasten them. Turn the cushion cover inside out with right sides together and sew the sides seams.
5. Turn the cushion cover out right side out and press the seams.

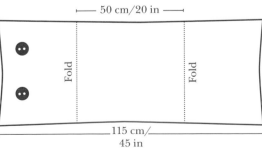
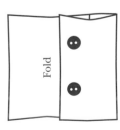

COFFEE CUP COVER
(page 115)

You will need: Damask tablecloth or other fabric; polyester wadding; quilting batting; lining fabric; buttons and decorative trimmings

Method

1. Photocopy the pattern for the coffee cup cover (size to fit). Place the sections on the outer fabric, which has been folded, and cut out. The seam allowance is included in the measurements.

2. Using the pattern pieces, cut out identical pieces from the lining fabric and the quilting batting, but cut these 2 cm (1 in) shorter than the outside edges of the pattern.

3. Sew the buttons to the outer fabric and decorate with trimmings before you sew the sections together.

4. Cut the handle out of a double layer of material, sew it together along the outer long edges, leaving the short ends open. Turn the handle right side out, stuff with wadding and sew it together at both ends.

5. Place the front and back sections right sides facing together, place the quilting batting on the wrong side and attach the handle as indicated in the photograph. Sew around the curved section and turn the work the right way round.

6. Sew around the curved section on the lining, pull it over the cover with right sides facing together and sew it together along the bottom. Be sure to leave an opening to turn the cover right side out.

7. Turn the cover right side out, and sew the opening together by hand. Push the lining inside the cover and press the seams.

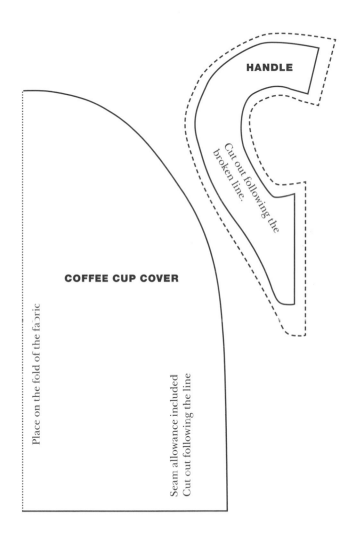

HANDLE

Cut out following the broken line.

COFFEE CUP COVER

Place on the fold of the fabric

Seam allowance included
Cut out following the line

EMBROIDERED TEA COSY
(pages 114–115)

You will need: Oval placemat in white-work embroidery; cotton wadding

Method
Cut the placemat across the middle and sew the sections together, with the wrong sides facing inside, along the curved edges. Make a lining of cotton wadding for the inside of the hood (cut it 2 cm/1 in smaller than the cover). Insert lining, fold a hem along the base of the hood, and sew along the hem by hand.

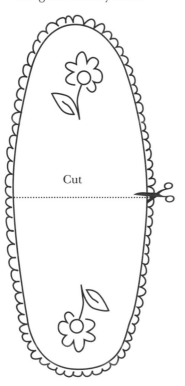

Cut

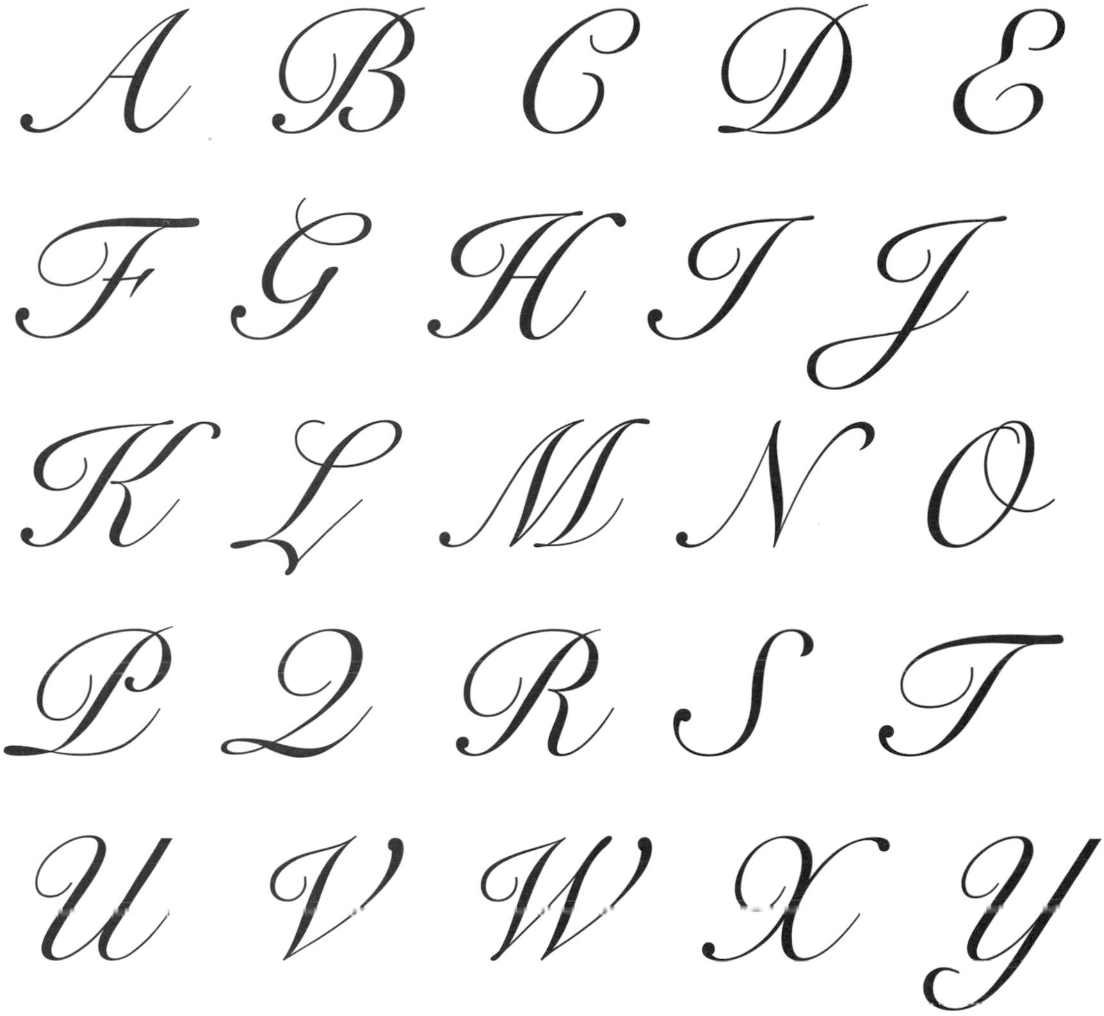

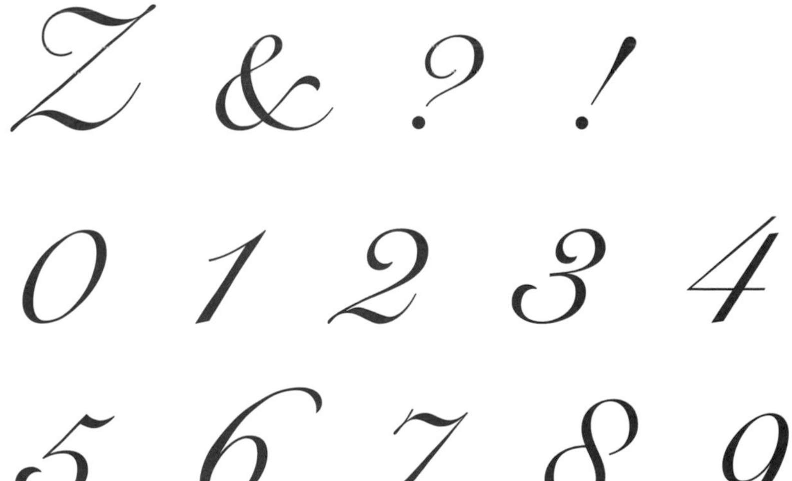

A B C D E

F G H I J

K L M N O

P 2 R S T

U V W X Y

Z & ? !

0 1 2 3 4   **STENCIL MOTIFS**

5 6 7 8 9

135

Sources

MATERIALS FOR RECYCLING

Check out
Architectural salvage materials at:
www.salvo.co.uk

Second-hand materials also available on:
www.ebay.co.uk

LETTERING STENCILS

Can be purchased at good stationers', art and craft shops, hobby shops or ordered online at:
www.stencilwarehouse.com
www.artifolk.co.uk

HOBBY MATERIALS

General hobby materials can be purchased at: branches of Hobbycraft or ordered online at:
www.hobbycraft.co.uk
www.hobby.uk.com
www.craftmaterialsupplies.co.uk
www.artdiscount.co.uk
www.craftsite.co.uk

Metal chandeliers, S-hooks, doorknobs, Kilner jars and old-fashioned milk bottles can be purchased from a number of sources, including mail-order catalogues, hardware and department stores and at IKEA branches − find details online at www.ikea.com

Batting, wadding and fabrics for patchwork and quilting can be ordered from:
www.cottonpatch.net
and many others available online

Appliqué materials, appliqué backing and embroidery threads can be ordered from:
www.gs-ukdirect.com
www.myfabrics.co.uk

Print transfer paper can be purchased at stationery shops or online at:
www.craftycomputerpaper.co.uk
www.creativetransfers.co.uk

Plaster-of-Paris and other moulding and modelling materials can be purchased from craft and hobby shops and are also available online from:
www.maragon.co.uk

Wax, wicks and other candle-making materials, as well as full instructions are available from hobby and craft shops and also available from:
www.candlemakingsupplies.co.uk
www.4candles.co.uk

Clock movements and hands are available from hobby and craft shops and can also be ordered from:
www.clockparts.co.uk
www.ycbclocks.co.uk

Tools and DIY materials can be purchased at hardware shops, DIY superstores, department stores or online at:
www.diy.com
www.homebase.co.uk

Wallpaper for decoupage and wrapping can be bought in most DIY shops, hardware stores etc. It can also be bought in some good department stores and also at branches of Laura Ashley or online at www.lauraashley.com

WE OWE THANKS TO MANY BUSINESSES AND ORGANIZATIONS WHO KINDLY LENT PROPS, ACCESSORIES AND MATERIALS FOR THIS BOOK INCLUDING:

Nitsirkna Design (www.nitsirkna.no)
Hegsbroveien 78, 3400 Lier, Norway
Thank you for lending the plate tower, the jewellery dish, the small stemmed dish and the fork chimes.

Dyhre Gård & Gartneri
Dyreveien 147, 1525 Moss, Norway

Fynd og klem
(www.fyndogklem.no)
Prinsens gate 6, 1530 Moss, Norway

Vollywood
(www.volleywood.no)
Arnestadveien 1, 1390 Vollen, Norway

Trekanten kjøpesenter
Knud Askers vei 26, 1383 Asker

Mosseporten kjøpesenter
Patterødvegen 2, 1599 Moss

Rortunct kjøpesenter
Stokkerveien 1, 3470 Slemmestad

SEVERAL FLORISTS PROVIDED THE CUT FLOWERS THAT APPEAR WITHIN THE BOOK INCLUDING:

Mester Grønn (www.mestergronn.no)

Trekanten Shopping Centre
Knud Askers vei 26, 1383 Asker, Norway

Mosseporten Shopping Centre
Patterødvegen 2, 1599 Moss, Norway

Rortunet Shopping Centre
Stokkerveien 1, Slemmestad, Norway

Index

Thanks

Many thanks to Ann Kristin and Ingunn at Gyldendal Publishers, Norway
– we enjoyed working together with you on our book.

Hanna Kristindóttir was born in Iceland and moved to Norway
to study interior design. She worked as an interior designer until
1998, when she began her career as a journalist with an interest in
crafts, hobbies and interior design.

Ellen Dyrop studied art at Oslo National Academy of Arts. She has
written many books on hobbies, crafts and interior design.

Their blog is at www.sjarmerende-gjenbruk.blogspot.com

Published in 2011 by New Holland Publishers (UK) Ltd
London • Cape Town • Sydney • Auckland

www.newhollandpublishers.com

Garfield House, 86–88 Edgware Road, London W2 2EA, United Kingdom

80 McKenzie Street, Cape Town 8001, South Africa

Unit 1, 66 Gibbes Street, Chatswood, NSW 2067, Australia

218 Lake Road, Northcote, Auckland, New Zealand

First published by Gyldendal Publishers AS, Norway, in 2009 as *Sjarmerende Gjenbruk*
© Gyldendal Norsk Forlag AS 2009. [All rights reserved]
© 2011 English translation, New Holland Publishers

A catalogue record for this book is available from the British Library

ISBN 978-1-84773-814-1 (PB)
ISBN 978-1-84773-924-7 (HB)

Publisher: Clare Sayer
Senior Editor: Marilyn Inglis
Cover and design: Ingunn Cecilie Jensen
Photographs: Helge Eek
Cover photographs: Helge Eek
Translation: Anne Bruce
Production: Laurence Poos

2 4 6 8 10 9 7 5 3 1

Reproduction by Pica Digital PTE, Singapore
Printed and bound in Malaysia by Times Offset (M) Sdn Bhd